M000164585

for Sara

it's the
little
things.

FINDING THE JOY IN THE SMALL THINGS IN LIFE

Sarah Ford

spruce

It is easy to find yourself just a little bit seduced by the big things, but it's the little things that will stay with you the longest, and they often come for free… These are the things that will add light and shade to your life and make you laugh – the icing on your cake.

What do you remember most about your best friend's wedding? Was it the expensive buffet, or the fact you danced all night with your friends? And what about that famous and fabulous restaurant you visited? Do you remember the extortionately priced food, or the fact that you drunkenly jumped in puddles with your bestie on the way home?

Maybe you like buying expensive new clothes, but how many of them sit in your wardrobe unworn? Isn't it so much better to go outside and throw a stick for your dogs? Would you rather read a brilliant book, found for pennies in a second-hand book store, or spend a small fortune on a magazine full of celebrity gossip?

Even when you're stuck in traffic and are late for work, it won't really matter. Not if you woke up that morning to the sound of birds singing outside, or your favourite song is playing on the radio.

No matter what is going on in the world, there is always joy to be found on your own doorstep.

Learn to laugh at the ridiculous, revel in your small achievements and delight in the mundane. Enjoy the calm while you can, stay up late and sleep in. If you find a pair of socks that are comfy and don't slide off your feet and into your shoes, go wild and buy seven pairs, one for each day of the week. Enjoy your sneezes, chuckle at your hiccups and laugh at the fact that the only time the cat wants to give you a kiss is right after it's licked its bum. Dance around your kitchen, celebrate a baking success, savour the smell of an expensive candle and giggle when you turn up in the same outfit as your friend.

And when you finally master the perfect eyeliner flick, you will know you can sleep well at night, as you will be forever glamorous. If it was good enough for Audrey it is good enough for you.

All of these things and more are the small things that make life joyful. They really are more important than the big things, as they make the very best memories. They are a reminder to stop stressing about life's problems and to start appreciating the little things instead.

The smell of a new book

Eating peanut butter
out of the jar

When a night out is
cancelled

Remembering your
password first time

Your favourite song
playing on the radio

Making new friends
· ·

Being home alone

Finding something amazing
in your mum's closet

The guilt-free glass
of wine after exercise

When the cat gives
you a kiss

When a parcel contains
bubble wrap

When your poached egg
is done to perfection

The smell of a
. . . .
scented candle
. . . .

Not having to shave your
legs in winter

Enjoying the wind
in your hair

Finding that essential
purchase at the supermarket

Wearing athleisure,
sporty and elastic -
always a winning combo

Creating the perfect
eyeliner flick first time

When it turns out that
your croissant has
chocolate in it

Feeling like a superhero
after a great day at work

A bathroom that has
. . . .
posh handwash
. . . .

When you've cooked just
the right amount of pasta

'Three-for-two' on your
favourite underwear

Taking your bra off
after a long day at work

Spotting a typo on a menu
....
#poopadoms
....

Resting your eyes
. . . .
for five minutes
. . . .

Getting the whole row
of seats on a plane...
let the vacation commence!

A successful day at
the sales

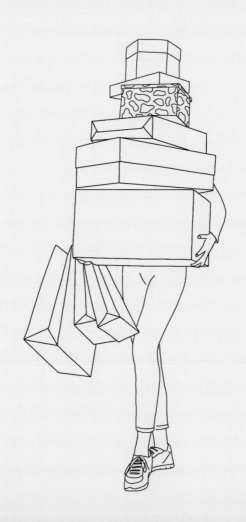

Making the most
of the sunshine

Spotting wildlife in
the city park

Finding a pen that works

first time

Finding a cashmere jumper
in a thrift store

Doing an online quiz and
finding out that your celeb
double is Audrey Hepburn

Enjoying a log fire

Losing yourself
in a big jumper

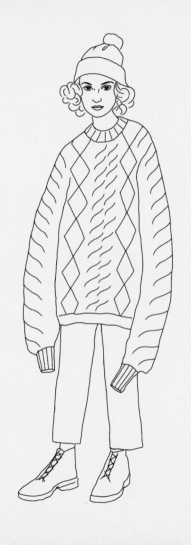

When the bus driver
waits for you

Dancing in the kitchen
with your nan

When someone hands you
some of their toilet roll

Turning up in the same
outfit as your bestie

Spotting your first
freckle of the year
- summer must be here

Pulling up to the pump
....
on the right side
....

Bumping into your ex when
you've just had a blow-dry

Finally reaching the floor
after weeks of yoga classes

Putting on your slippers
at the end of the day

An Hachette UK Company
www.hachette.co.uk

First published in Great Britain in 2020 by Spruce,
an imprint of Octopus Publishing Group Ltd
Carmelite House
50 Victoria Embankment
London EC4Y 0DZ
www.octopusbooks.co.uk

Text copyright © Sarah Ford 2020
Design, layout and illustration copyright © Octopus Publishing Group Ltd 2020

Distributed in the US by
Hachette Book Group
1290 Avenue of the Americas
4th and 5th Floors
New York, NY 10104

Distributed in Canada by
Canadian Manda Group
664 Annette St.
Toronto, Ontario, Canada M6S 2C8

All rights reserved. No part of this work may be reproduced or utilized in
any form or by any means, electronic or mechanical, including photocopying,
recording or by any information storage and retrieval system, without the
prior written permission of the publisher.

Sarah Ford asserts the moral right to be identified as the author of this work.

ISBN 978-1-84601-590-8

A CIP catalogue record for this book is available from the British Library.

Printed and bound in China

10 9 8 7 6 5 4 3 2 1

Commissioned by: Ella Parsons
Art Director: Juliette Norsworthy
Illustrator: Agnes Bicocchi
Designer: Geoff Fennell
Senior Production Manager: Katherine Hockley